199
THINGS
EVERY
AMERICAN
SHOULD KNOW

AMERICAN HERITAGE MAGAZINE

American Heritage, A Division of Forbes Inc., New York, N.Y.

TABLE OF CONTENTS

INTRODUCTION

How precise is the educated American's understanding of the history of our country? I don't mean exact knowledge of minor dates, or small details about the terms of laws, or questions like "Who was secretary of war in 1851?" *(Answer:* Charles M. Conrad.) But just how well does the average person remember the important facts—the laws, treaties, people, and events that should be familiar to everyone?

What follows is not a test; nor are these items necessarily the most important things to know about American history. But these are all things an American-educated person might reasonably be expected to be familiar with. Most of them can be found in my college textbook *The American Nation* or in any similar work. A good secondary school teacher might mention any of them in the course of a lecture or class discussion.

If you have never heard of most of these items, either you have a particularly poor memory or teachers like me have not accomplished what we set out to do. On the other hand, if you already know that, in addition to being President Millard Fillmore's secretary of war, Charles M. Conrad killed a man in a duel (according to the *Dictionary of American Biography,* he was "very intense in his convictions and tenaciously persistent in support of whatever cause he espoused") and served at various times in both houses of the United States Congress and in the Confederate Congress, you don't have to read another word: you know about everything I have to say here—and a lot more. But for the majority of readers, here are 199 things you *should* know about American history.

John A. Garraty is Chairman of the Department of History at Columbia University and a contributing editor to American Heritage magazine. His most recent book, *1001 Things That Everyone Should Know About American History,* is published by Doubleday.

POLITICS MAKES GOOD SLOGANS

1 **TIPPECANOE AND TYLER TOO.** Used by the Whig party in 1840, when William Henry Harrison, the hero of the Battle of Tippecanoe, was the Whig presidential candidate, and John Tyler his running mate. The battle, fought in 1811 in Indiana, destroyed the Indian confederacy organized by Tecumseh, a Shawnee chief, and his brother, Tenskwatawa, known as the Prophet.

2 **54°40′ OR FIGHT.** A Democratic rallying cry in the 1844 presidential campaign, referring to the dispute over whether the United States or Great Britain owned the Pacific Northwest, which had been under joint control since 1818. American expansionists, led by the Democratic presidential candidate, James K. Polk, demanded that the United States take over the entire region, which extended to 54°40′ north latitude. In 1846 President Polk agreed to a compromise dividing the region at the 49th parallel.

3 **VOTE YOURSELF A FARM.** Refers to the Republican party's promise in the 1860 campaign to give land in the West to anyone who would settle on it. Unlike so many campaign promises, this one was kept, by passage of the Homestead Act of 1862.

4 **DON'T SWAP HORSES IN THE MIDDLE OF THE STREAM.** First used by Republicans to persuade voters to reelect Abraham Lincoln in 1864.

Hoover button, 1932.

5 **WE DID NOT GO TO WAR.** A phrase used by Martin Henry Glynn, a former governor of New York, in the keynote speech at the 1916 Democratic Convention, which nominated Woodrow Wilson for a second term. When it and other references to Wilson's success in maintaining neutrality drew thunderous applause, the Democrats decided to stress that argument in the fall campaign.

6 EVERY MAN A KING. The slogan of the Louisiana senator Huey Long's Share Our Wealth movement during the Great Depression. Long proposed to confiscate all fortunes of more than five million dollars and all incomes of more than one million dollars, and to use the money to give every American family a house, a car, and an annual income of two thousand dollars or more.

7 A CHICKEN FOR EVERY POT. (And a car in every garage.) Used by the Republicans in the 1928 presidential campaign to suggest what they liked to call "Coolidge prosperity."

8 HAD ENOUGH? The question was asked by the Republicans during the 1946 congressional elections. After fourteen years of "Democratic rule," the Republicans maintained, it was "time for a change."

9 A CHOICE, NOT AN ECHO. The postwar rallying cry of conservative Republicans opposed to nominating Republicans who favored accepting most New Deal reforms. When, in 1964, the conservatives succeeded in nominating Barry Goldwater for President, they made wide use of the slogan "In your heart you know he's right," prompting Democrats to retort . . .

10 . . . IN YOUR GUTS, YOU KNOW HE'S NUTS.

11 A PUBLIC OFFICE IS A PUBLIC TRUST. This 1884 Democratic campaign slogan reminded voters that the Republican candidate ("Blaine, Blaine, James G. Blaine, the continental liar from the state of Maine") was believed to have sold favors to a railroad while Speaker of the House in the 1870s.

The 1884 slogan as used in 1892.

12 WE DO OUR PART. The motto of NRA, the New Deal's National Recovery Administration, was used in conjunction with the famous Blue Eagle emblem to identify the products of companies that had adopted NRA codes of fair business practices.

13 NIXON'S THE ONE. Republican slogan in the 1968 presidential campaign, sometimes used by the Democrats on posters bearing the photograph of a very pregnant black woman.

THEY SHOT THE PRESIDENT

14 JOHN WILKES BOOTH shot and killed Lincoln in a Washington theater in April 1865. Booth was a rabid Confederate sympathizer who believed slavery was "one of the greatest blessings . . . God ever bestowed upon a favoured nation."

15 CHARLES J. GUITEAU shot President James Garfield in Washington's Union Station on July 2, 1881, and the President died of his wounds two months later. Guiteau's reason was not, as had often been claimed, that he was a disappointed office seeker, but on the order (he insisted) of "the Deity." Guiteau was, however, an admirer of the New York senator Roscoe Conkling, leader of the Republican faction, who had clashed with Garfield over patronage questions.

16 LEON F. CZOLGOSZ, an anarchist, shot and killed William McKinley in 1901, while McKinley was shaking hands on a reception line at the Pan-American Exposition in Buffalo, because he was against all government and because "I didn't believe one man should have so much services and another man should have none." Almost certainly neither Garfield nor

McKinley's assassin, Czolgosz.

McKinley would have died of his wounds if modern medical techniques had been available.

17 JOHN F. SCHRANK shot the former President Theodore Roosevelt as TR was leaving a hotel in Milwaukee on his way to make a speech during his Bull Moose campaign in 1912. Though fired at point-blank range, the bullet passed through a folded copy of Roosevelt's hour-long speech and his glasses case before lodging just short of his lung. (If he had been less prolix, he might well have been killed.) Roosevelt insisted on going ahead with the speech before being taken to a hospital. He also insisted that Schrank was not insane, since he had made the attempted assassination in a state that had no death penalty. "I may gravely question," TR later wrote an English friend, "if he has a more unsound brain than Senator La Follette or Eugene Debs."

18 LEE HARVEY OSWALD shot and killed John F. Kennedy in 1963, but his motive cannot be determined, nor for that matter can his responsibility for the murder be settled beyond question, since he himself was killed by one Jack Ruby before he could be brought to trial.

Lee Harvey Oswald,
in custody.

19 JOHN W. HINCKLEY, JR., shot and seriously wounded Ronald Reagan and three members of his party in March 1981 outside a Washington hotel because Hinckley wished to impress Jodie Foster, an actress for whom he had developed a secret passion after seeing her in a movie. The day of the shooting he wrote, but did not mail, a letter to her saying, "The reason I'm going ahead with this attempt now is because I just cannot wait any longer to impress you." Hinckley, who was acquitted on the grounds of insanity, is also alleged to have told someone in Texas that "as far as he was concerned, politicians should be eliminated."

SEVEN SUPREME COURT DECISIONS

20 MARBURY v. MADISON (1803). William Marbury sued Secretary of State James Madison in order to obtain a commission appointing him a justice of the peace that had been signed but not delivered by retiring President John Adams. Important because in deciding the case, the Court for the first time declared a law of Congress unconstitutional.

21 McCULLOUGH v. MARYLAND (1819). John W. McCullough, cashier of the Baltimore branch of the Bank of the United States, was sued by Maryland because he refused to pay a tax levied on the bank by the state legislature. The case is notable because, in deciding it in favor of the bank, Chief Justice John Marshall interpreted the powers of Congress broadly. The Constitution did not specifically grant Congress the right to create a bank, but a bank was a reasonable way for Congress to exercise powers enumerated in the document. "Let the end be legitimate," Marshall declared, "and all means which are appropriate . . . are constitutional." Since the bank was constitutional and since the Constitution was the supreme law, the state tax on the bank was unconstitutional because "the power to tax involves the power to destroy."

22 GIBBONS v. OGDEN (1824). Thomas Gibbons and Aaron Ogden were rival ferryboat operators. Ogden had been granted the exclusive right to operate a ferry between New York City and New Jersey by New York State, but Gibbons set up a competing line. When Ogden sued, the Supreme Court

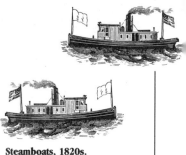

Steamboats, 1820s.

decided that the New York law was unconstitutional because it interfered with interstate commerce, a prerogative of the federal government. By defining commerce as "intercourse" (and not merely as the movement of goods), the Court laid the basis for the later federal regulation of navigation, radio, and television, and other forms of transportation and communication.

23 MUNN v. ILLINOIS (1876). This case involved the refusal of Ira V. Munn, a Chicago grain-elevator operator, to obey an 1871 Illinois law regulating the practices of railroads, warehouses, and similar businesses providing services to the public. The Court upheld the Illinois law and seven other similar state laws, ruling that "when private property is devoted to a public use, it is subject to public regulation."

24 PLESSY v. FERGUSON (1896). Homer Adolph Plessy, a light-skinned Louisiana black man, was arrested for sitting in a railroad car reserved by Louisiana law for whites. In a New Orleans court his lawyers argued that the law was unconstitutional, but Judge John H. Ferguson ruled against them, on the ground that the railroad had provided separate but equally good cars for blacks, as the law required. This line of reasoning was upheld by the Supreme Court. The case is remembered today mainly for the dissent of Justice John Marshall Harlan. "Our Constitution is color-blind," Harlan wrote. "The arbitrary separation of citizens, on the basis of race . . . is a badge of servitude wholly inconsistent with civil freedom."

25 BROWN v. BOARD OF EDUCATION OF TOPEKA (1954). This is the famous school-desegregation case in which the Court unanimously overturned *Plessy v. Ferguson.* "In the field of public education," Chief Justice Earl Warren stated, "the doctrine of 'separate but equal' has no place."

Linda Brown of Topeka, Kansas.

26 ROE v. WADE (1973). Norma McCorvey (or Jane Roe), a woman prevented from having an abortion by a Texas law, sued to have the law overturned. Henry Wade, a Dallas district attorney, pushed the case up to the Supreme Court. Texas claimed that the case should have been dismissed as moot, since the plaintiff had already had her baby. In a controversial decision the Court ruled in McCorvey's favor, establishing the right of women to have abortions during the early months of pregnancy.

THE WORST SUPREME COURT DECISION

27 DRED SCOTT v. SANDFORD (1857). A slave, Dred Scott sued for his freedom on the ground that his master, an Army surgeon, had taken him into Illinois and then the Wisconsin Territory, where slavery had been barred by Congress in the Missouri Compromise. The Court, whose majority decision was read by Chief Justice Roger B. Taney, ruled that the Missouri Compromise was unconstitutional because it violated the property rights protected by the Fifth Amendment, since it denied slave owners the right to take their property wherever they wanted to. In effect, this decision opened all the West to slavery, infuriated the North, and pushed the nation more precipitously toward civil war.

Chief Justice Roger Taney.

I DON'T KNOW HIM FROM ADAMS

28 SAMUEL ADAMS (1722–1803), organizer of the Sons of Liberty and the Boston Tea Party, signer of the Declaration of Independence, governor of Massachusetts.

JOHN ADAMS (1735–1826), cousin of Samuel, one of the drafters of the Declaration of Independence, a negotiator of the peace treaty ending the Revolution, first Vice-President and second President of the United States.

Samuel

ABIGAIL SMITH ADAMS (1744–1818), wife of John, manager of the family properties during long periods when he was away on public business. Popular with modern feminists, especially for having urged John to "remember the ladies" while helping to create the new nation.

Abigail

JOHN QUINCY ADAMS (1767–1848), son of John and Abigail, diplomat, senator, President of the United States, and, late in life, member of the House of Representatives.

CHARLES FRANCIS ADAMS (1807–86), son of John Quincy, vice-presidential candidate of the Free Soil party in 1848, congressman, minister to Great Britain during the Civil War, editor of the papers of John and of John Quincy.

Charles Francis

CHARLES FRANCIS ADAMS, JR. (1835–1915), son of Charles, Union officer, historian, railroad executive, public official.

HENRY ADAMS (1838–1918), second son of Charles Francis, Sr., historian, editor, teacher, novelist, author of *The Education of Henry Adams.*

Henry

BROOKS ADAMS (1848–1927), another son of Charles, Sr., historian, philosopher, professional pessimist.

John

John Quincy

C.F., Jr.

Brooks

GOOD PHRASES FOR BIG ISSUES

29 THE GREAT WAR FOR THE EMPIRE. The name given for what is more commonly known as the Seven Years' War by the historian Lawrence Henry Gipson in his monumental *The British Empire before the Revolution* (1936–67). Gipson's point was that what Americans know as the French and Indian War was part of a worldwide struggle between France and Great Britain for control of vast areas in America and Asia.

30 THE AMERICAN SYSTEM. A scheme designed by Henry Clay in the 1820s. Clay sought to form a coalition of Eastern and Western interests in Congress. In return for Western support of protective tariffs that would benefit Eastern manufacturers, the Easterners would vote for bills providing federal expenditures on roads and canals.

31 THE PECULIAR INSTITUTION. A Southern euphemism for slavery. The term was not intended to be a pejorative; by "peculiar" Southerners meant particular or unique, not odd or queer.

32 WAVING THE BLOODY SHIRT. This post–Civil War Republican tactic involved reminding Northern voters that the South was made up mostly of Democrats and that many Northern members of that party had been at best lukewarm about resisting secession. The term came into use after the congressman Benjamin F. Butler displayed before his colleagues the bloodstained shirt of a Northerner who had been flogged in Mississippi. The

A *Puck* cover.

"bloody shirt" was used by Republicans for decades as a way of diverting attention from politically embarrassing contemporary issues. A classic speech in this vein was given by Robert G. Ingersoll in the campaign of

13

1880: "Every man that lowered our flag was a Democrat. Every man that bred bloodhounds was a Democrat. Every preacher that said that slavery was a divine institution was a Democrat. Recollect it! Every man that shot a Union soldier was a Democrat. Every wound borne by you Union soldiers is a souvenir of a Democrat."

33 MANIFEST DESTINY. This term, coined by John L. O'Sullivan in 1845 in an article in his *United States Magazine and Democratic Review,* reflected the expansionist spirit of the era. It was, O'Sullivan wrote, "our *manifest* [read 'obvious'] *destiny* to overspread the continent."

34 THE ROBBER BARONS. This name was applied to the ultrarich industrialists of the late nineteenth century, such as the railroad magnates Cornelius Vanderbilt and Jay Gould, and the oil tycoon John D. Rockefeller. It originated in the late 1860s but became a symbol for corporate power and the evils of unrestrained economic freedom only with the publication of Matthew Josephson's best seller *The Robber Barons* in 1934.

Robber Barons, as seen by *Puck*.

TWENTY WONDERFUL NICKNAMES

35 HIS ROTUNDITY. John Adams, so called because of his shape.

36 OLD HICKORY. Andrew Jackson, because of his toughness. The name dates from his days as an Indian fighter during the War of 1812. After the Battle of Horseshoe Bend in

14

Alabama in 1814, his Creek Indian foes gave him another name, "Sharp Knife."

37 THE LITTLE MAGICIAN. Martin Van Buren (also called "The Red Fox" and "The American Talleyrand"), because he was a crafty and inventive political manager. His New York machine was known as the Albany Regency because, during the 1820s and 1830s, it ran things while Van Buren spent most of his time away in Washington as senator, Secretary of State, Vice-President, and finally President.

38 HIS ACCIDENCY. John Tyler, so called after he succeeded to the Presidency upon the death of William Henry Harrison in 1841. Since this was the first time a President had died in office, there was some question as to the extent of Tyler's authority.

39 OLD FUSS AND FEATHERS. Gen. Winfield Scott, like his contemporary Zachary Taylor, was a successful soldier (more, however, as an organizer and strategist than as a battlefield leader). Scott earned this nickname by being extremely vain and something of a blusterer.

40 OLD ROUGH AND READY. Zachary Taylor was given this name by his troops during his long career in the Army, because of his informal yet confidence-building way of dealing with them and his rough-hewn appearance.

A Taylor scarf, 1848 election.

41 THE LITTLE GIANT. Stephen A. Douglas (also called "The Steam Engine in Britches"), because of his short stature (he had a massive head and trunk perched on stubby, almost dwarfish legs), his colorful personality, and his self-confident political style.

42 THE PLUMED KNIGHT. James G. Blaine, so called by his many Republican admirers; the Democrats called him other things. The name was bestowed on Blaine by Robert Ingersoll, a spellbinding orator of the era, in a speech nominating him for President at the 1876 Republican Convention. The nomination, however, went to . . .

43 . . . **HIS FRAUDULENCY.** Rutherford B. Hayes, who won the Presidency in the famous disputed election of 1876. Hayes's wife, who would not allow liquor in the White House, was known as "Lemonade Lucy."

44 **THE PATHFINDER.** John C. Fremont, because of his long career as an explorer and surveyor, and his excellent published reports on his explorations, written with the help of his wife, Jessie, the daughter of Sen. Thomas Hart Benton.

45 **THE GREAT COMMONER.** William Jennings Bryan (also called "The Boy Orator of the Platte" and "The Peerless Leader"), because of his stress on being a product of and a representative of "the people." When the free-silver issue surfaced in the 1890s, Bryan, then in the House of Representatives, announced: "The people of Nebraska are for free silver. Therefore I am for free silver. I'll look up the reasons later."

46 **THE ROUGH RIDER.** Theodore Roosevelt (also called "TR" and "Teddy," which latter name he disliked intensely), because of the regiment of that name, composed of a motley mixture of cowboys, adventurers, and odd characters raised by Roosevelt to fight in the Spanish-American War.

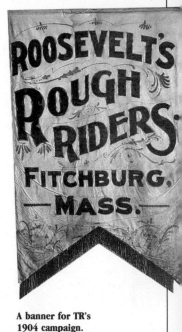

A banner for TR's 1904 campaign.

47 **THE OHIO ICICLE.** Sen. John Sherman of Ohio, sponsor of the Sherman Antitrust Act, because of his stiff, colorless personality. Sherman is thought to have invented the political term "to mend some fences."

48 **BIG BILL.** William Howard Taft, because he weighed more than three hundred pounds.

49 **SILENT CAL.** Calvin Coolidge, who had little to say and said it economically—*e.g.,* "The business of America is business" and, when asked if he would seek reelection in 1928, "I do not choose to run."

50 **THE HAPPY WARRIOR.** Alfred E. Smith, who was given this name by Franklin D. Roosevelt in the course of a speech nominating him for President at the 1924 Democratic Convention.

51 **THE KINGFISH.** Huey P. Long, because of his total dominance of his native state of Louisiana.

52 **TAIL GUNNER JOE.** Joseph R. McCarthy, the Communist-hunting senator who claimed—falsely—to have been a tail gunner on American bombers during World War II.

53 **TRICKY DICK.** Richard M. Nixon, because of his shifty, calculating political style. The phrase long antedated the Watergate scandal.

54 **LANDSLIDE LYNDON.** Lyndon B. Johnson, because of the paper-thin margin by which he won Texas's Democratic primary for the Senate in 1948.

SEVEN SPEECHES TO REMEMBER

55 **GEORGE WASHINGTON'S FAREWELL ADDRESS** (1796), in which he stressed the importance of national unity as the "main pillar" of the nation's independence, peace, and prosperity.

56 THOMAS JEFFERSON'S FIRST INAUGURAL ADDRESS (1801), which contains his famous reference to the United States as "the world's best hope" and his praise of "wise and frugal government which shall restrain men from injuring one another, [and] shall leave them otherwise free to regulate their own pursuits." At the time, the fact that Jefferson's election marked the first real change of party control of the government made his promise to respect the rights of the Federalist minority seem the most important point in the address.

57 DANIEL WEBSTER'S SECOND REPLY TO HAYNE (1830), in which he called the American flag "the gorgeous ensign of the republic" and concluded with the sentence: "Liberty *and* Union, now and forever, one and inseparable." Webster's grandiloquence was much admired by contemporaries, but the speech was actually important because of its powerful refutation of the passionate but confused argument of South Carolina's

Webster replies to Hayne, 1830.

Senator Robert Y. Hayne that the separate states were the ultimate source of sovereignty in the American political system.

58 ABRAHAM LINCOLN'S "HOUSE DIVIDED" SPEECH (1858), delivered on the occasion of his nomination as the Republican candidate for senator from Illinois. This was probably Lincoln's most radical statement about the implications of the slavery issue, the one in which he predicted that "this government cannot endure permanently half slave and half free." It got him in some trouble with Northern conservatives, especially when opponents quoted the remark out of context in order to suggest that Lincoln was an abolitionist. Lincoln did not, in this speech or on any other occasion before the war, call for the abolition of slavery.

59

WILLIAM JENNINGS BRYAN'S "CROSS OF GOLD" SPEECH at the 1896 Democratic National Convention. Bryan, arguing for a plank in the party platform calling for the free coinage of silver, ended with the sentence "You shall not press down upon the brow of labor this crown of thorns, you shall not crucify mankind

A broadside of Bryan and family.

upon a cross of gold." "You" were the Gold Democrats, the supporters of the incumbent President, Grover Cleveland, who opposed the unlimited coinage of silver. The speech made a national figure of the thirty-six-year-old Bryan and led to his nomination for the Presidency by the convention.

60

WOODROW WILSON'S CALL FOR DECLARATION OF WAR AGAINST GERMANY (1917), which contains the famous line "The world must be made safe for democracy." The speech is remarkable for Wilson's insistence that "we have no quarrel with the German people. . . . We fight without rancor and without selfish object." Such forbearance and Wilson's promise that victory would result in a "universal dominion of right" helped win liberal support for the war effort, but it contributed to postwar disillusionment when his idealistic hopes were not realized.

61

FRANKLIN D. ROOSEVELT'S FIRST INAUGURAL ADDRESS (1933), remembered for the line "the only thing we have to fear is fear itself," for Roosevelt's promise "to put people to work," and perhaps for use of the phrase "good neighbor" when referring to foreign policy. It was an extraordinarily effective speech, but it also contained a good deal of windy political foolishness, and a considerable amount of bad advice. For example, the President felt it necessary to point out that "happiness lies not in the mere possession of money"; he promised to balance the federal budget and urged state and local governments to reduce their expenditures "drastically";

and he claimed that there was an "overbalance of population" in the nation's cities.

TEN PAINTINGS THAT SAY 'AMERICA'

62 PAUL REVERE,
by John Singleton Copley
(painted in 1765–70).

63 THE DECLARATION OF
INDEPENDENCE,
by John Trumbull (1786–97).

64 GEORGE WASHINGTON,
by Gilbert Stuart. The
"unfinished" version (1796).

65 EXHUMING THE MASTODON,
by Charles Willson Peale
(1801).

66
RAFTSMEN PLAYING CARDS,
by George Caleb Bingham
(1847).

67
THE GROSS CLINIC,
by Thomas Eakins
(1875).

68
THE GULF STREAM,
by Winslow Homer
(1886).

69
STAG AT SHARKEY'S,
by George Bellows
(1907).

70
AMERICAN GOTHIC,
by Grant Wood
(1930).

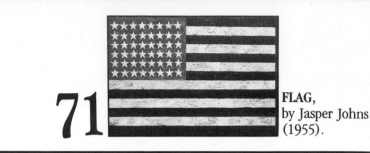

71 FLAG,
by Jasper Johns
(1955).

QUOTATIONS WORTH QUOTING

72 "I heard the bullets whistle, and, believe me, there is something charming in the sound." (George Washington, writing to his brother after his first experience in battle, in 1754. When the letter was published in Great Britain, King George II is said to have remarked that the young soldier would not have found the sound so charming "if he had been used to hearing more.")

73 "O! ye that love mankind! Ye that dare oppose not only the tyranny but the tyrant, stand forth!" (Thomas Paine, urging the colonies to declare their independence, in *Common Sense,* 1776.)

74 "Sell [our] country! Why not sell the air, the clouds, and the great sea?" (Tecumseh, resisting suggestions that the Indians cede their lands in the Ohio Country to the United States, 1810.)

75 "Don't give up the ship!" (Capt. James Lawrence after being mortally wounded in the battle between the USS *Chesapeake* and the HMS *Shannon,* 1813.) A somewhat fuller version of the line runs, "Tell the men to fire faster and not to give up the ship; fight her till she sinks."

76 "The mass of mankind has not been born with saddles on their backs, nor a favored few booted and spurred, ready to ride them legitimately, by the grace of God." (Thomas Jefferson, letter to Roger C. Weightman, 1826.)

77 "The American continents, by the free and independent condition which they have assumed and maintained, are henceforth not to be considered as subjects for future colonization by any European powers." (James Monroe enunciating the Monroe Doctrine in his annual message to Congress, 1823).

78 "The politicians of New York are not so fastidious as some gentlemen are, as to disclosing the principles on which they act. They boldly preach what they practice. . . . If they are defeated, they expect to retire from office. If they are successful, they claim, as a matter of right, the advantages of success. They see nothing wrong in the rule that to the victor belong the spoils of the enemy." (Sen. William L. Marcy, defending Jackson's appointment of Martin Van Buren as minister to Great Britain, 1831.)

79 "The history of mankind is a history of repeated injuries and usurpations on the part of man toward woman, having in direct object the establishment of an absolute tyranny over her." (Elizabeth Cady Stanton and Lucretia Mott, "Declaration of Sentiments" at the Woman's Rights Convention, Seneca Falls, New York, 1848.)

80 "If I could save the Union without freeing any slave, I would do it; and if I could save it by freeing *all* the slaves, I would do it; and if I could do it by freeing some and leaving others alone, I would do that. . . . I have here stated my purpose according to my *official* duty, and I intend no modification of my oft-expressed *personal* wish that all men, everywhere, could be free." (Abraham Lincoln, replying to the appeal of editor Horace Greeley [August 1862] that he emancipate the slaves.)

81 "It is well that war is so terrible—we should grow too fond of it." (Gen. Robert E. Lee, speaking to Gen. James Longstreet during the Battle of Fredericksburg, 1863.)

82 "The man of wealth [should] consider all surplus revenues which come to him simply as trust funds, which he is called upon to administer . . . to produce the most beneficial results for the community—the administer, doing for them better than they would or could do for themselves." (Andrew Carnegie, "Wealth," 1889.)

83 "To those of my race who depend on bettering their condition in a foreign land or who underestimate the importance of cultivating friendly relations with the Southern white man, who is their next-door neighbor, I would say, 'Cast down your bucket where you are.' " (Booker T. Washington, speaking at the Atlanta Cotton States and International Exposition, 1895.)

84 ". . . Mr. Washington apologizes for injustice, he belittles the emasculating effects of caste distinctions, and opposes the higher training and ambitions of our brighter minds. . . . The way for people to gain their reasonable rights is not by voluntarily throwing them away." (W.E.B. Du Bois, "Of Mr. Booker T. Washington and Others," 1903.)

85 "The main element of any United States policy toward the Soviet Union must be that of long-term, patient but firm and vigilant containment of Russian expansive tendencies." ("X" [George F. Kennan], "The Sources of Soviet Conduct," 1947.)

The Soviet emblem since 1923.

86 "In the councils of government, we must guard against the acquisition of unwarranted influence, whether sought or unsought, by the military-industrial complex. The potential for the disastrous rise of misplaced power exists and will persist." (President Dwight D. Eisenhower, 1961.)

87 "I'm not a crook." (President Richard M. Nixon, 1973.)

Richard Nixon in close-up.

SOME FAMOUS THINGS
THEY DIDN'T SAY

88 "Caesar had his Brutus; Charles the First his Cromwell; and George the Third [The Speaker: 'Treason!']...." (Patrick Henry attacking the Stamp Act in the Virginia House of Burgesses, 1765.) Henry did say something like this, though no copy of his speech exists. But he almost surely did not add *"may profit by this example. If this* be treason, make the most of it." The evidence that he said that consists of the recollections of eyewitnesses recorded nearly half a century later. The only contemporary account claims that "henery," when interrupted by the Speaker, "said that if he had affronted the speaker, or the house, he was ready to ask pardon, and he would show his loyalty to his majesty, King G. the third, at the Expense of the last drop of his blood."

89 "Entangling alliances." A phrase often incorrectly said to come from George Washington's Farewell Address. Washington warned not against "entangling" alliances but against both "passionate attachments" and "inveterate antipathies" to particular foreign countries. It was Thomas Jefferson who said, in his first Inaugural, "peace, commerce, and honest friendship with all nations, entangling alliances with none."

90 "Millions for defense, but not one cent for tribute." Charles Cotesworth Pinckney was supposed to have said this in 1797 when he and two other American diplomats who were trying to negotiate a treaty with the French were asked for a bribe by agents of the foreign minister Talleyrand. What Pinckney did say was, "No! No! Not a sixpence, sir!" The famous words, however, were spoken a year later by Congressman Robert Goodloe Harper of South Carolina at a banquet for another of these diplomats, John Marshall.

91 "The only good Indian is a dead Indian." Attributed to Gen. Philip Sheridan, who in fact said something only slightly less objectionable: "The only good Indians I ever saw were dead."

92 "Lafayette, we are here" was not said by General Pershing upon setting foot on French soil at the head of the first contingents of the American Expeditionary Forces in 1917. It was said by an aide, Charles E. Stanton.

93 "Prosperity is just around the corner." Though often attributed to Herbert Hoover, the former President always denied having used the phrase. Actually there was nothing fatuous in the statement, even if Hoover had made it. Well into 1931 most people believed the Depression would be short. Hoover claimed that his enemies were twisting a statement he made in 1930: "I am convinced we have passed the worst and with continued effort we will rapidly recover."

94 "What's good for General Motors is good for the country." This quote is only partially correct. What Charles E. Wilson, former head of General Motors, actually said in testifying before the Senate committee considering his nomination in 1952 to be Secretary of Defense was a bit different: "What is good for the country is good for General Motors, and what's good for General Motors is good for the country."

KNOW THESE SIX GREAT HISTORIANS (BECAUSE THEY'RE OUR BEST)

95 GEORGE BANCROFT—because his ten-volume *History of the United States* (published 1834–74) was the first detailed account from the discovery to the end of the Revolution, based on archives in America and Europe. Bancroft was also Secretary of the Navy and minister to Great Britain in the Polk administration and minister to Prussia after the Civil War.

96 FRANCIS PARKMAN— because his multivolume history (1851–92) of France's exploration and colonization of North America and of the Franco-British struggle for control of the continent is one of the most gripping narrative histories in the English language. Although Parkman had many prejudices (he considered Indians untrustworthy savages and

An 1897 drawing of Parkman.

Catholics undemocratic), his enormous work, completed despite years of fragile health and near-blindness, is both beautifully written and factually accurate.

97 HENRY ADAMS—(one of *the* Adamses, see item 28)— because his *History of the United States during the Administrations of Jefferson and Madison* (1889–91) is still a major source for the period. In addition Adams taught at Harvard, where he sponsored the first history Ph.D.'s granted by the university, and wrote other important works of history, two novels, and his autobiography, *The Education of Henry Adams* (1918).

98 FREDERICK JACKSON TURNER—because his essay "The Significance of the Frontier in American History" (1893), which stressed the way the frontier experience had affected American development, was a major influence on the writing of all American history for more than half a century.

Frederick Jackson Turner, 1906

99 CHARLES A. BEARD—because his controversial *An Economic Interpretation of the Constitution* (1913) put an end to the view of the Founding Fathers as demigods by emphasizing that the Constitution they created benefited them financially. Beard is also important because his *The Rise of American Civilization* (1927–42), written with his wife, Mary, provided a gripping narrative account of American development that stressed economic, intellectual, and social aspects.

100 ALLAN NEVINS—because, besides training more than a hundred Ph.D.'s and writing dozens of excellent historical works on subjects ranging from the Civil War to Henry Ford, which won him two Pulitzer Prizes, a National Book Award, and numerous other honors, he was a lifelong advocate of the writing of good popular history, and one of the founders of American Heritage.

ONE DATE EVERYONE GETS WRONG

101 It seems almost everyone is unable to remember the year—or even the decade—in which Congress enacted the Missouri Compromise. It was 1820. The compromise admitted Missouri to the Union as a slave state and Maine as a free one, but it also divided the rest of the land obtained from France by the Louisiana Purchase into slave and free territory at 36°30' north latitude, Missouri's southern boundary. Although this legislation satisfied moderates for a generation, by mid-century the slavery issue was becoming ever more intense.

It was addressed again by the Compromise of 1850; the 1820 act itself was repealed by the Kansas-Nebraska Act of 1854, which permitted the residents of those territories to decide the slavery question for themselves. Passed in the forlorn hope of maintaining peace, the new legislation instead triggered bloody civil war in Kansas Territory between proslavery and antislavery settlers.

The violence of the 1850s throws the hopeless compromises of that decade into high relief and makes us less aware of the earlier measure.

WHAT'S NEW?

102 NEW SOUTH. A term used after the Civil War by Southern publicists and boosters of industrial development in the region as a kind of shorthand for modernization and economic expansion.

103 NEW FREEDOM. The program of Woodrow Wilson in the 1912 presidential campaign, a counter to Roosevelt's New Nationalism. It urged the country to rely on competition rather than government regulation to protect the public against economic exploitation. Monopolistic corporations should be broken up by strict enforcement of the antitrust law. Then the competition of the "freed" smaller companies would keep costs and prices down and profits reasonable.

104 NEW NEGRO. A term used in the decade after World War I by black intellectuals of the Harlem Renaissance, who stressed racial pride and independence from white influences. In *The New Negro* (1925) the educator and critic Alain Locke urged

THE NEW NEGRO

A stylized African motif from the 1925 anthology.

blacks to exchange "the status of beneficiary and ward for that of a collaborator and participant in American civilization."

105 NEW ERA. The Republican description of the mid-1920s, when wages, profits, and stock prices were on the rise, interest rates were low, and business leaders seemed the embodiment of wisdom and good citizenship. During the New Era, the advertising executive Bruce Barton described Jesus Christ in all seriousness as "the founder of modern business."

106 NEW LEFT. A 1950s British term, adopted by American radicals in the 1960s, mostly young, who bitterly opposed racism, the Vietnam War, corporate power, and "middle-class" morality. The term was used as a pejorative by many people.

107 THE NEW IMMIGRATION. This term was used by opponents of unrestricted immigration to distinguish the change that occurred in the flow of European immigrants to the United States beginning in the 1880s. Whereas previously the majority had come from northern and western Europe, the "new" immigrants came from southern and eastern sections of the Continent. People who made the distinction claimed that the newcomers were either "unfit" or incapable of being assimilated in the American "melting pot."

PHRASES THAT GRABBED US

108 O GRAB ME. The word *embargo,* spelled backward. The term was concocted by opponents of the Embargo Act of 1807, which sought to deal with the impressment of American sailors on the high seas and other violations of the rights of neutrals during the Napoleonic Wars by forbidding virtually all exports to "any foreign port or place."

109 CORRUPT BARGAIN. A charge made by supporters of Andrew Jackson before and during the 1828 presidential campaign. In 1824 none of the four candidates won a majority in the Electoral College, but Jackson had the largest total, ninety-nine. John Quincy Adams had eighty-four; William H. Crawford, forty-one; and Henry Clay, thirty-seven. The election was therefore thrown into the House of Representatives, where Clay used his influence to swing the election to Adams. When Adams then appointed Clay his Secretary of State, Rep. George Kremer charged that a "corrupt bargain" had been made.

110 BLEEDING KANSAS. Name applied by abolitionists and other opponents of slavery to the chaotic situation that developed in the Kansas Territory in the mid-1850s. With the territory open to slavery as a result of the Kansas-Nebraska Act, pro- and antislavery supporters rushed to the state to try to capture the government. Fighting broke out between proslavery "Border Ruffians" from Missouri and antislavery settlers. John Brown's raid at

Pottawatomie is the best known of the numerous atrocities of the period.

111 **COTTON IS KING.** Argument of Southern disunionists in the 1850s, who claimed that the North would not resist secession because its economy and that of Great Britain and other European powers were dependent on Southern cotton.

112 **SEWARD'S FOLLY.** The response of critics of Secretary of State William H. Seward's purchase of Alaska from Russia in 1867, who felt that the price, $7,200,000, was far too high.

113 **LET'S GET ANOTHER DECK.** This was a Republican response in 1936 to Franklin Roosevelt's New Deal. When that failed, the Republicans tried *Two Good Terms Deserve a Rest.* This rather feeble 1940 slogan met, of course, with equal lack of success.

114 **TWISTING THE LION'S TAIL.** A nineteenth-century political technique involving criticism of Great Britain in general and British policies in particular in order to win the support of Irish-Americans.

115 **REMEMBER THE MAINE.** Rallying cry of those eager to go to war with Spain in order to free Cuba after the USS *Maine* blew up in Havana Harbor in February 1898.

116 **PERDICARIS ALIVE OR RAISULI DEAD.** This phrase (actually a telegram sent by Secretary of State John Hay to the sultan of Morocco) was used by the Republicans to help elect Theodore Roosevelt in 1904. Ion Perdicaris and his son had been abducted in Morocco by a bandit named Ahmed ibn-Muhammed Raisuli. The Greek-born

A monument in Key West to the *Maine* and her crew.

Perdicaris, whose American citizenship was actually open to question, was released before Hay's telegram arrived.

117 KEEP COOL WITH COOLIDGE. Republican advice during the 1924 presidential campaign, probably an attempt to make a virtue of Calvin Coolidge's taciturn style.

118 MASSIVE RETALIATION. Secretary of State John Foster Dulles's substitute for the Democrats' policy of "containing" Soviet expansion. Dulles proposed that any Soviet or Red Chinese aggression should be nipped in the bud by threatening to respond with nuclear weapons. This "atomic diplomacy" was also said to offer the United States the cheapest possible defense—a "bigger bang for a buck."

119 ALL THE WAY WITH LBJ. The Democratic slogan in 1964 urging that Lyndon B. Johnson—who had become President after Kennedy's assassination the year before— deserved to be elected in his own right.

120 IT'S MORNING IN AMERICA AGAIN. A phrase used by Republican publicists in the 1984 election to describe the apparent change of mood in the country from pessimism to optimism.

TEXTS THAT CHANGED OUR LIVES

121 COMMON SENSE (1776), by Thomas Paine. The pamphlet that, with its bold call for outright independence rather than reform of the British imperial system and with its harsh attack on both King George III, the "Royal Brute," and the very idea of monarchy, persuaded thousands to favor a complete break with Great Britain.

122 UNCLE TOM'S CABIN (1852), by Harriet Beecher Stowe. Whether or not Abraham Lincoln actually said to Stowe, "So this is the little woman who made this big war," this book had an enormous impact on how

Northerners felt about slavery. It did so principally because of Stowe's ability to describe plantation slaves as individual people with deep feelings caught in an evil system without treating every white character in the story as an unmitigated villain.

Poster advertising "an edition for the millions" of Stowe's novel.

123 THE INFLUENCE OF SEA POWER UPON HISTORY (1890), by Alfred Thayer Mahan. Captain Mahan argued that nations with powerful navies and the overseas bases to support them were victorious in war and prosperous in peacetime. The book had a wide influence among American military and political leaders.

124 WEALTH AGAINST COMMONWEALTH (1894), by Henry Demarest Lloyd. This powerful, if somewhat exaggerated, attack on the Standard Oil monopoly attracted wide attention. In addition to denouncing Standard's business practices—Lloyd said that the trust had done everything to the Pennsylvania legislature except refine it—he denounced laissez-faire economics and the application of Darwinian ideas about survival of the fittest to social affairs.

125 THE SCHOOL AND SOCIETY (1899), by John Dewey. In this book the author developed the basic ideas of what was later to be known as "progressive" education. Schools should build character and train children to be good citizens, not merely provide them with new knowledge. They should make use of the child's curiosity, imagination, and past experience, not rely on discipline and rote memory to teach.

126 THE JUNGLE (1906), by Upton Sinclair. Sinclair's story of the life of a Chicago stockyard worker described both the filthy conditions under which cattle were slaughtered and the ways in which the meat packers exploited their workers. The novel was a best seller and led, partly because President Theodore Roosevelt reacted to it by setting in motion a government investigation, to federal meat inspection and the passage of the Pure Food and Drugs Act of 1906.

127 SEXUAL BEHAVIOR IN THE HUMAN MALE (1948), by Alfred C. Kinsey. This study, based on more than five thousand interviews with men of all ages, and a similar volume on women, published in 1953, demonstrated that people of all kinds engaged in a great variety of sexual practices. The books had an enormous influence on public attitudes toward human sexuality.

128 THE OTHER AMERICA (1962), by Michael Harrington. This book was a major force behind the so-called War on Poverty of the Lyndon Johnson era. Harrington called attention to what he called the "invisible land." Forty or fifty million souls, "somewhere between 20 and 25 percent of the American people," were living below the poverty line, he claimed. Most of them were crowded into inner-city slums, "invisible" to the middle class.

129 SILENT SPRING (1962), by Rachel Carson. By showing how pesticides such as DDT affected birds and other animals, and indirectly humans, too, *Silent Spring* caused a public furor that led to the banning of many such substances and to the modern attack on all forms of pollution.

Rachel Carson, ecologist and author.

130 THE FEMININE MYSTIQUE (1963), by Betty Friedan. If this work did not give birth to the modern feminist movement, it surely raised it to maturity. Friedan argued that most of the opinion-shaping forces of modern society were engaged in a witless effort to convince women of the virtues of domesticity. By so doing, they were wasting the talents of millions. Women should resist these pressures. "The only way for a woman . . . to know herself as a person," wrote Friedan, "is by creative work."

ROCKEFELLERS

131

JOHN D. ROCKEFELLER (1839–1937), organizer of the Standard Oil trust, principal benefactor of the University of Chicago, billionaire, *bête noire* of the antimonopolists. Also founder of the Rockefeller Institute for Medical Research, the Rockefeller Foundation "to promote the well-being of mankind," and other charitable organizations, and longtime Baptist Sunday school superintendent of Cleveland.

WILLIAM ROCKEFELLER (1841–1922), brother of John D., oilman, Wall Street promoter, a director of the National City Bank, public utility magnate and railroad man, *bon vivant.*

JOHN D. ROCKEFELLER, JR. (1874–1960), son of John D., founder of Rockefeller University and the Cloisters, builder of Riverside Church and Rockefeller Center in New York City, restorer of Colonial Williamsburg and other historic sites, contributor of the land on which the United Nations headquarters stands, teetotaler. Father of Winthrop, David, Laurance, John D. III, and Nelson.

ABBY ALDRICH ROCKEFELLER (1874–1948), wife of John D., Jr., and daughter of Sen. Nelson Aldrich of Rhode Island; a founder and benefactor of the Museum of Modern Art.

JOHN D. ROCKEFELLER III (1906–78), first president of the Rockefeller Brothers Fund, a founder of both the Lincoln Center for the Performing Arts and the Asia Society.

BLANCHETTE HOOKER ROCKEFELLER (1909–), wife of John D. III, art collector, president and chairman of the Museum of Modern Art.

NELSON ALDRICH ROCKEFELLER (1908–79), coordinator of Inter-American Affairs under Franklin Roosevelt, Assistant Secretary of State, Undersecretary of the Department of Health, Education, and Welfare, four-term Republican governor of New York, three-time seeker of the Republican presidential nomination, Vice-President of the United States.

LAURANCE S. ROCKEFELLER (1910–), philanthropist, businessman, conservationist.

WINTHROP ROCKEFELLER (1912–73), Republican governor of Arkansas, closely involved in development of Colonial Williamsburg.

DAVID ROCKEFELLER (1915–), international banker, chairman of Chase Manhattan Bank, philanthropist, public official.

JOHN D. ROCKEFELLER IV (1937–), son of John D. III and Blanchette, Democratic senator and governor of West Virginia, diplomat.

TEN MORE WONDERFUL NICKNAMES

132 CAPTAIN SHRIMP. The name given to Miles Standish of the Plymouth Colony by his enemy Thomas Morton of Merry Mount. The reference, of course, was to his diminutive stature.

133 LIGHT-HORSE HARRY. The nickname of Henry Lee, Revolutionary War cavalry officer, friend of Washington, and father of Robert E. Lee. It was Henry Lee who described Washington as "first in war, first in peace, and first in the hearts of his countrymen."

134 CHAMPAGNE CHARLIE. Charles Townshend, British chancellor of the exchequer, who pushed the Townshend Acts (taxing tea, glass, paint, paper, and other products imported to the colonies) through Parliament in 1767.

135 MAGNUS APOLLO. DeWitt Clinton, longtime mayor of New York, governor of New York, United States senator, unsuccessful Federalist candidate for President in 1812; so called because of his large size and impressive appearance. Despite the many offices he held, Clinton's most important achievement was his planning and carrying to completion in 1825 the 363-mile-long Erie Canal.

136 SLOW TROT. The Civil War Union general George H. Thomas, so called because of his careful, seemingly unimaginative way of organizing for battle. He was actually a brilliant tactician and battlefield commander, as is demonstrated by his better known nickname, *The Rock of Chickamauga,* given to him after his troops withstood a furious Confederate assault in that battle.

137 YOUNG NAPOLEON. Union general George B. McClellan, so called because he somewhat resembled *the* Napoleon in physical appearance and grandiose style, and because of his inflated sense of his own importance.

138 BIG BILL. William Dudley Haywood, the radical leader of the Western Federation of Miners, who in 1905 was a founder of the Wobblies, the Industrial Workers of the World, an organization noted for violent strikes and an anticapitalist philosophy.

139 HONEY FITZ. John Fitzgerald, Boston political boss, best known for being the grandfather of his namesake, John Fitzgerald Kennedy. Fitzgerald got the name for his charm and skill at singing "Sweet Adeline." He was also known as *Fitzblarney,* for more easily understandable reasons.

140 PECK'S BAD BOY. Title was given to President Woodrow Wilson by unscrupulous political opponents because of his supposed illicit relationship with a divorcée, Mrs. Mary Allen Peck.

141 BLACK JACK. The name given Gen. John J. Pershing by West Point cadets because of the strict discipline he maintained while assigned there in the late 1890s. Pershing had earlier commanded the 10th Cavalry, an all-black unit, and was devoted to that regiment. This roused the scorn of the cadets.

LAND OF REBELS

142 BACON'S REBELLION, 1676. An uprising of western Virginia planters against the Eastern Establishment headed by Sir William Berkeley, the royal governor. The Westerners, led by Nathaniel Bacon, resented both the social pretensions of the Berkeley group—which in turn considered the Baconites "a giddy and unthinking multitude"—and Berkeley's unwillingness to support their attacks on local Indians. Bacon raised a small army, murdered some peaceful Indians, burned Jamestown, and forced the governor to flee. But Bacon came down with a "violent flux" and died, and soon thereafter Berkeley restored order.

143 LEISLER'S REBELLION, 1689–91. After news of the abdication of James II had reached New York, Jacob Leisler, a local militia captain, proclaimed himself governor of the colony. He claimed to rule in the name of the new monarchs, William and Mary, and attempted without success to organize an expedition against French Canada during King William's War. In 1691, after a governor appointed by King William had arrived in New York, Leisler resisted turning over power. He was arrested, tried for treason, and executed.

144 PAXTON BOYS UPRISING, 1763–64. Pennsylvania frontiersmen—many of them from the town of Paxton—angered by the Eastern-dominated colonial Assembly's unwillingness to help in the defense against Indian attacks, murdered some peaceful Indians (always easier than taking on warlike tribes) and marched on Philadelphia. They were persuaded to return to their homes by a group headed by Benjamin Franklin, who promised the Assembly would authorize paying bounties for Indian scalps.

145 PONTIAC'S REBELLION, 1763–64. Indians of the Great Lakes area, led by Pontiac, chief of the Ottawas, attempted unsuccessfully to drive the British out of their territory and check the influx of white settlers who invaded the region after the end of the French and Indian War.

Pontiac smoking a peace pipe with Maj. Robert Rogers.

146 REGULATOR WAR, 1769–71. Another east-west conflict, this one in North Carolina, triggered by the dominance of the eastern counties. It culminated in the Battle of Alamance, where a thousand government troops beat a "Regulator" (rebel) force twice that size.

147 SHAYS' REBELLION, 1786–87. This Massachusetts uprising was both a result of unstable economic conditions following the Revolution and an important cause of the movement to strengthen the central government that resulted in the drafting of the Constitution. Debt-ridden western Massachusetts farmers, led by Daniel Shays, seeking to stop foreclosures and obtain the printing of new issues of paper money by the state, marched on Springfield, where they hoped to seize a government arsenal. Government militia units easily defeated them, however, and Shays fled the state. The "rebellion" then collapsed.

148 WHISKEY REBELLION, 1794. When Congress enacted a stiff excise tax on whiskey in 1791, farmers in western Pennsylvania were especially hard hit. They were accustomed to turning their surplus grain into whiskey, which was much easier to store and ship to market than grain

Washington reviews troops called up in 1794.

itself. When the farmers organized protest meetings and prevented the collection of the tax, President Washington announced that their actions "amount to treason" and ordered them to disperse, When they did not, he called up thirteen thousand militiamen (more men than he had ever commanded during the Revolution) and marched against them. Faced with this overwhelming force, the protesters submitted. Thomas Jefferson, who was popular throughout the West, had the tax repealed after he became President in 1801.

149 DORR'S REBELLION, 1841–42. Long after the Revolution, Rhode Island continued to function under a charter dating from the seventeenth century that restricted the suffrage to substantial landowners and their eldest sons. More than half the adult male population (and all the women) did not have the right to vote. When the legislature refused to remedy this situation, a People's party led by Thomas W. Dorr, a well-to-do lawyer, drafted a constitution and submitted it to a popular vote. It was overwhelmingly approved, and the People's party then elected Dorr governor. Of course, the existing government did not recognize these actions. The legal governor proclaimed martial law and sent militia units against the Dorrites. Dorr surrendered and was convicted of treason. He was sentenced to life imprisonment but released a year later.

150 ANTIRENT WAR, 1839–46. A protest movement occasioned by the attempt of Hudson Valley landlords to collect what amounted to feudal dues based on "leases" dating from the colonial period. In 1839, after the death of Stephen Van Rensselaer III, who owned about three thousand farms and was "owed" some four hundred thousand dollars in back rents, his heirs attempted to collect these debts. Van Rensselaer had been lax about these obligations, and the tenants resorted to violence to prevent foreclosures. The New York State militia was called out, and order was restored. In 1844 a legislative committee decided that the Van Rensselaer titles were legal. This caused farmers, disguised as Indians, to riot again. After a sheriff had been killed by the antirenters, martial law was again declared, and order restored. Finally, in 1846, a new state constitution put an end to the old tenures, and eventually the tenants obtained title to their farms.

CARTOONS

151

A plea by Benjamin Franklin for colonial unity against the French, this 1754 woodcut from the Pennsylvania *Gazette* may have been the first cartoon to appear in an American newspaper.

152

The gerrymander entered the political bestiary in 1812 via this cartoon decrying partisan district apportionment in Massachusetts under Gov. Elbridge Gerry.

A WISE ECONOMIST ASKS A QUESTION

153

In 1931, the year this Pulitzer Prize–winning cartoon by John T. McCutcheon appeared, more than two thousand banks failed and unemployment reached eight million.

COME ON IN, I'LL TREAT YOU RIGHT. I USED TO
KNOW YOUR DADDY

154

This 1937 cartoon by C.D. Batchelor reflected the isolationist sentiment of the time. By 1937, when the Nazis were arming, Japan had invaded China, and the Spanish Civil War had erupted, a poll showed that 94 percent of the people opposed American involvement in any war.

155

Daniel Fitzpatrick's prophetic 1955 cartoon depicted the United States advancing toward a heart of darkness.

THREE MORE THINGS THEY DIDN'T SAY

156

"Why don't you speak for yourself, John?" There is no record that Miles Standish asked John Alden to propose to Priscilla Mullens or any other female Pilgrim in his behalf, and since John and Priscilla may have been married as early as 1621, the story told by Longfellow in

"The Courtship of Miles Standish" is no doubt an example of poetic license.

157

"**I wish some of you would tell me the brand of whiskey that Grant drinks. I would like to send a barrel of it to every one of my other generals.**" Lincoln was supposed to have said this to a delegation of politicians who had complained to him of Grant's drinking. Lincoln, however, denied having made the remark, saying, "That would have been very good if I had said it," and on another occasion: "No, I didn't happen to say it—but it's a good story, a hardy perennial. I've traced that story as far back as George II and General Wolfe. When certain persons complained to George that Wolfe was mad, George said, 'I wish he'd bite some of the others!'"

158

"**Fighting Joe,**" Civil War general Hooker's nickname, was not given him because of his bold, aggressive tactics, though he was anything but a cautious commander. During General McClellan's 1862 campaign against Richmond, a last-minute Associated Press dispatch reached the New York *Courier and Enquirer* just as the paper was going to press. It began: "Fighting— Joe Hooker," meaning that what followed was to be added to earlier accounts of the action involving Hooker's

Maj. Gen. Hooker resigned his command before Gettysburg.

corps. The compositor, however, set it up as a heading, "Fighting Joe Hooker," and after publication the name caught on. Hooker claimed not to like the name, saying, "It sounds like Fighting Fool," and "People will think I am a highwayman or bandit."

IT'S A PANIC

Nowadays we call "ordinary" economic downturns "recessions": in early times they were called "panics." There have been a lot of them:

159 PANIC OF 1819. In 1819 the boom that had followed the War of 1812 ended. The downturn that ensued was triggered by the revival of European agriculture after the ending of the Napoleonic Wars and by the contraction of credit instituted by the Second Bank of the United States, which was paying off loans that had been made to finance the Louisiana Purchase. Sales of undeveloped land on the frontier then slowed to a trickle, and the price of cotton and other crops dropped sharply. Many farmers were unable to pay their debts, and this led to foreclosures and to numerous bank failures. The bad times lasted until about 1822. Although the Bank of the United States was not really responsible for the troubles, many Westerners blamed it. Among them was Andrew Jackson, who took his revenge, so to speak, by vetoing a bill to extend the charter of the bank in 1832. Ironically, this set in motion events that led to the . . .

160 PANIC OF 1837. The transfer of federal money from the conservative Bank of the United States to the "wildcat" state banks after President Jackson had vetoed the bill extending the charter of the bank enabled the wildcats to make credit available on easy terms. This led to soaring land sales in the West (up from $2,600,000 in 1832 to $24,900,000 in 1836) and an accompanying boom in canal and road construction, the latter largely financed by British investors. But in 1836 Jackson issued the Specie Circular, which required purchasers of government land to pay for it with gold or silver. This caused purchasers to withdraw specie from the banks and to buy less land. The banks' loss of gold and silver reserves in turn led to the restriction of credit and to many bank failures. The panic occured when every bank in the country had to suspend converting its paper currency into specie on demand. Conditions improved thereafter, and in 1838 the banks resumed specie payments; but the revival was short-lived. The economy remained depressed until 1843.

161

PANIC OF 1857. This downturn was the result of falling grain prices caused by a big increase in Russian exports of wheat after the Crimean War. As a result, Western farmers could buy less, and their declining consumption hurt the business of both Eastern manufacturers and the

The run on Seamen's Bank, October 1857.

railroads. The bankruptcy of the Ohio Life Insurance and Trust Company in August 1857 was followed by the collapse of many hundreds of rural banks. The Southern states were hurt less by the bad times because the European demand for cotton remained high. This strengthened Southerners' confidence in the viability of their slave economy.

162

PANIC OF 1873. The failure of the banking house of Jay Cooke and Company precipitated this panic, which was by far the most severe one up to that date. The New York Stock Exchange had to be shut down for ten days to check the steep decline of prices. But like all others, the causes of the following economic downturn, which lasted for several years, were complex. Dislocations caused by the Civil War played a part, but more important were the reckless overbuilding of American railroads and the

The crowd at the New York Stock Exchange, September 18, 1873.

opening of the Suez Canal, which caused major readjustments in world trade patterns. The year 1873 also marked the beginning of a period of severe worldwide price deflation that extended far beyond the bad times of the mid-1870s.

163 PANIC OF 1893. Triggered by the failure of the National Cordage Company in May and marked by many bank failures and business bankruptcies later in the year, this panic exacerbated an already serious economic decline. The causes were worldwide, but in the United States the conflict over the coinage of silver, which was advocated by groups hurt by the long deflationary cycle, was a major factor. The Treasury's declining gold reserves, which fell below a hundred million dollars (considered a danger point), further eroded public confidence in the economy. The next few years were among the darkest in American history, being marked by the Pullman Strike, in which federal troops were used to keep the trains running, widespread protest marches by unemployed people, and the spectacle of the government's having to turn to a private banker, J.P. Morgan, to obtain enough gold to avoid bankruptcy. The question of the free coinage of silver seems less important today than it did in the 1890s, but it split the Democratic party, gave force to the Populist movement, and made a national figure of William Jennings Bryan.

164 PANIC OF 1907. This was known as the "rich man's panic." In October the failure of F. Augustus Heinze's United Copper Company led to runs on a number of banks. When depositors suddenly began to withdraw money in huge amounts from the Knickerbocker Trust Company, whose president had been associated with Heinze, the bank had to close its doors. This precipitated a full-fledged panic. The hero of the resulting crisis was the same J.P. Morgan who had been pictured as a villain during the depression of the 1890s. Morgan rallied other bankers to raise cash to help hard-pressed but sound institutions to withstand the pressure of frightened

J.P. Morgan

depositors and to bolster sagging prices on the stock exchange. President Theodore Roosevelt helped by authorizing the deposit of federal funds in New York banks to bolster their reserves. The President also agreed to allow U.S. Steel to swallow the Tennessee Coal and Iron Company in order to save the brokerage house that owned it, a decision he was later to regret. The long-range effect of the panic on the economy was not great, but it led to important reforms, notably the creation of the Federal Reserve System in 1913–14.

165 PANIC OF 1929. This was the famous "Black Thursday," the stock market collapse of October 24, 1929. The trend of securities prices had been down for several weeks, when suddenly the market gave way. Although it certainly had a psychologically depressing effect on millions of people, the Crash, as it was called, did not cause the depression that followed. By the end of the year stock prices had regained a good part of what had been lost in October, and it was only in the spring of 1930 that the serious economic downturn began. What was remarkable about the resulting depression was its length and the persistent high unemployment.

SEVEN FAMOUS WARSHIPS

166 BONHOMME RICHARD. Forty two guns, flagship of Capt. John Paul Jones during the Revolution. In a bloody battle off the east coast of England in 1779, the *Bonhomme Richard* defeated the vastly more powerful *Serapis.* Early in the engagement, when asked if he had struck his colors, Jones replied, "I have not yet begun to fight."

Outgunned, aflame, yet victorious.

167 CONSTITUTION. During the War of 1812, while under the command of Capt. Isaac Hull, the heavy frigate *Constitution* defeated HMS *Guerrière.* Later in the war, while commanded by William Bainbridge, the *Constitution* destroyed HMS *Java.* She was known as Old Ironsides. The *Constitution* is still a commissioned warship in the U.S. Navy and can be visited today at the Boston Navy Yard.

168 ALABAMA. A Confederate warship, powered by steam and sail, that was built during the Civil War in England. Between July 1862, when she was put to sea, and her destruction in a battle with the USS Kearsarge in

A Confederate raider's last battle.

June 1864 in the English Channel off Cherbourg, the *Alabama* captured or destroyed more than sixty Union ships. In 1872 arbitrators awarded the United States $15,500,000 in compensation for damage to its shipping done by the *Alabama* and two other Confederate raiders built in England during the war.

169 MONITOR. Built in desperate haste to counter the Confederate ironclad *Merrimack,* the *Monitor* was the revolutionary creation of the engineer John Ericsson. Above a submerged hull, she mounted two big guns in a revolving turret. When she arrived in Hampton Roads, Virginia, in March 1862, a Rebel officer said she was the "strangest looking craft we had ever seen . . . an immense shingle floating in the water with a gigantic cheese box rising from its center." But she fought her foe to a standstill in a duel that marked the beginning of the end of the wooden warships.

170 OREGON. This 1896 battleship is best known for its epic fifteen-thousand-mile voyage from its base on the Pacific coast around South America to the West Indies in order to be available in case of war with Spain over Cuba. The vessel accomplished its object and played a major role in the destruction of the Spanish

The *Oregon* in 1898.

fleet after the war had started. But the time the trip took, well over two months, was one of the reasons the United States undertook the construction of the Panama Canal.

171 GREER. This old four-stacker destroyer fired the first American shots of World War II in September 1941. While en route to Iceland, the *Greer* received a message from a patrolling British plane that it had sighted a German submarine nearby. The *Greer* made sonar

The *Greer* off New York, 1943.

contact with the U-boat and began to trail it. After the British plane had dropped four depth charges in the area and the *Greer* continued to follow its maneuvers closely, the U-boat fired a torpedo at the destroyer. The *Greer* dropped a total of nineteen depth charges in an unsuccessful effort to sink the sub. In announcing the engagement, President Franklin D. Roosevelt ordered the Navy to attack German vessels in the North Atlantic on sight. "When you see a rattlesnake poised to strike," he said, "you do not wait until he has struck before you crush him." Roosevelt neglected to inform the public, however, that the *Greer* had been pursuing the submarine when it struck.

172 PT-109. Speedy but frail, this patrol torpedo boat became famous because, at the time it was cut in two in the black of an August night in 1943 by the Japanese destroyer *Amagiri,* it was commanded by Lt. (jg.) John F. Kennedy.

FIVE BLACK "TROUBLEMAKERS"

173 DENMARK VESEY (ca. 1767–1822) was a slave who purchased his freedom after winning a lottery and organized an elaborate uprising among South Carolina slaves. However, the authorities got wind of the scheme, and Vesey and thirty-five other blacks were hanged, despite the fact that no actual uprising had taken place.

174

SOJOURNER TRUTH (ca. 1797–1883) was a leading black abolitionist in the decades before the Civil War, unusual in that she campaigned for women's rights as well as for the ending of slavery. At a women's rights convention in 1851 she said: "The man over there says women need to be helped into carriages and lifted over ditches, and to have the best place everywhere. Nobody ever helps me into carriages or over puddles, or gives me the best place—and ain't I a woman? . . . I have ploughed and planted and gathered into barns, and no man could head me—and ain't I a woman?"

Sojourner Truth in 1853.

175

FREDERICK DOUGLASS (ca. 1817–95), a Baltimore slave, escaped to New York in 1838. He became an abolitionist, developed an extraordinary ability as a speaker, and published an abolitionist paper, the *North Star*. During the Civil War he helped raise black regiments and in later life continued to campaign for full equality for blacks and for women.

176

MARCUS GARVEY (1887–1940), an ardent black nationalist, founded the Universal Negro Improvement Association. By the mid-1920s the association had nearly a million members and Garvey had created the Black Star steamship line and other all-black businesses. He hoped to establish an independent black nation in Africa the success of which would compel whites to accept blacks as equals. Eventually,

Black nationalist Marcus Garvey.

however, his companies failed and he was convicted of fraud and deported to his native Jamaica.

177 MALCOLM X (1925–65), born Malcolm Little, was a "hustler" who was converted to the Black Muslim faith while in prison. Having become one of the most radical Muslim critics of white America, a black nationalist who opposed integration of any sort on the ground that white people were devils, he began to moderate his position after extensive travels in the Middle East and Africa. His career was cut short when he was assassinated after he had begun to criticize other Muslim leaders.

WOMEN ON WOMEN

178 "[Men] denied us the means of knowledge and then reproached us for the want of it. . . . They doomed the sex to servile or frivolous employment on purpose to degrade their minds, that they themselves might hold unrivalled the power and preemptions they usurped." Priscilla Mason, 1793.

179 "There is no foundation in reason or expediency, for the absolute and slavish subjection of the wife to the husband, which forms the foundation of the present legal relations. Were woman, in point of fact, the abject thing which the law, in theory, considers her to be when married, she would not be worthy the companionship of man."
Lucretia Mott, 1849.

180 "Men call us angels, and boast of the deference they pay to our weakness! They give us their seats in church, in cars and omnibusses, at lectures and concerts, and in many other ways show us great respect where nothing but form is concerned. . . . but at the same time they are defrauding us of our just rights by crowding us out of

Amelia Bloomer, feminist and fashion innovator.

every lucrative employment, and subjecting us to virtual slavery." Amelia Bloomer, 1851.

181 "The reason why women effect so little & are so shallow is because their aims are low, marriage is the prize for which they strive, if foiled in that they rarely rise above the disappointment. . . . But we feel this so keenly we now demand an equal education with man to qualify us to become co-workers with him in the great arena of human life." Sarah Grimk, "Education of Women," 1852–57.

182 "Southern women are I believe all at heart abolitionists. I will stand to the opinion that the institution of slavery degrades the white man more than the Negro and exerts a most deleterious effect upon our children." Ella Thomas, a Georgian, writing in her journal, 1858.

183 "Women have the same invaluable right to life, liberty, and the *pursuit* of happiness that men have. Why have they not this right politically as well as men? Women constitute a majority of the people of this country—they hold vast portions of the nation's wealth and pay a proportionate share of the taxes. . . . The American nation, in its march onward and upward, cannot publicly choke the intellectual and political activity of half its citizens by narrow statutes." Victoria Woodhull, testifying before the House Judiciary Committee, 1871.

184 "A Woman's body belongs to herself alone. It does not belong to the United States of America or any other government on the face of the earth." Margaret Sanger, *Woman Rebel,* 1914.

185 "Even the woman movement we have called feminism has not succeeded by and large in giving women any control over men. It has only changed the distribution of women . . . removing vast numbers of women from the class supported by men to the class working for them." Elsie Clews Parsons, *Social Rule,* 1916.

186

"With women as half the country's elected representatives, and a woman President once in a while, the country's *machismo* problems would be greatly reduced. . . . I'm not saying that women leaders would eliminate violence. We are not more moral than men; we are only uncorrupted by power so far." Gloria Steinem, 1970.

Women Now!

A 1969 poster.

LET'S MAKE A DEAL

In an intensely competitive political society where 55 percent is a sweeping victory and 60 percent a landslide, success in politics often depends upon the art of compromising. American history is therefore full of wheeling and dealing, where one group agrees to something it dislikes in order to get something that it wants very much or, to put a better face on the practice, where politicians take into account the needs of others as well as themselves and try to do what is best for the entire country. Apart from the Missouri Compromise of 1820 and the Compromise of 1850 (see Item 101), here are some examples:

187

THE GREAT COMPROMISE (1787). This was the agreement reached at the Constitutional Convention between the smaller, less populous states, which wished all states to be represented equally in Congress, and the larger states, which favored representation according to population. The compromise, of course, was to give each state two senators, chosen by its legislature, and to apportion seats in the House of Representatives according to population and elect the members by popular vote. The Great Compromise was far less important than the Founding Fathers thought at the time, since in practice most issues have divided the country on economic or geographic lines, not on the size of the states.

188

THE THREE-FIFTHS COMPROMISE (1787). This was a deal at the convention between Northern and Southern delegates. Northerners wanted to count slaves as property in the apportionment of federal taxes. Southerners wanted to count them as part of the population when

A twentieth-century rendition of the 1787 Constitutional Congress.

determining the size of each state's delegation in the House of Representatives. The compromise was to count each slave as three-fifths of a person for both purposes. In practice this favored the South because no direct taxes were enacted by Congress until after slavery was abolished.

189

THE COMPROMISE TARIFF (1833). In the late 1820s and early 1830s Northern and Western interests had pushed laws through Congress placing high protective duties on many imported manufactured goods. Most Southerners disliked these duties because there was little manufacturing in their section. Passage of the Tariff of 1832 led South Carolina (inspired by its leading statesman, John C. Calhoun) to enact an Ordinance of Nullification declaring that law and the previous tariff void in South Carolina and prohibiting the collection of duties in the state after February 1, 1833. To prevent the showdown between state and federal authority that would have followed, Calhoun and Henry Clay (whose American System had encouraged the coalition of Northern and Western interests that had made passage of the high tariffs possible) engineered the passage of a new tariff that lowered the duties gradually over a period of years. South Carolina then repealed its ordinance before the February 1 deadline.

190

THE CRITTENDEN COMPROMISE (1860). This proposal was advanced by Sen. John J. Crittenden of Kentucky, a disciple of Henry Clay, who had died in 1852, to relieve the sectional crisis that resulted from the election of Lincoln as President. Crittenden suggested a constitutional amendment allowing slavery in all territories south of 36°30' and guaranteeing that no future amendment would seek to tamper with slavery where it already existed. The necessary legislation failed, however, when Republicans refused to go along with any extension of slavery into new territory.

191 THE COMPROMISE OF 1877. This deal broke the deadlock created by the disputed 1876 presidential election. In exchange for accepting the Republican version of the results and thus the election of Rutherford B. Hayes, the Democrats were promised that Hayes would remove the last Federal troops from the South and appoint a Southerner to his cabinet. The compromise marked the end of the Reconstruction Era and of Federal efforts to compel white Southerners to treat blacks fairly.

192 THE ATLANTA COMPROMISE (1895). The name given to the policy proposed by Booker T. Washington in his speech at the Atlanta Cotton States and International Exposition. Washington urged Southern blacks to accept segregation and to concentrate on developing useful skills. In return he urged white Southerners to help black people get ahead in the world. If they did, he promised, blacks would be the "most patient, faithful, law-abiding, and unresentful people that the world has seen." The policy worked in the sense that it reduced racial tensions and attracted considerable Northern philanthropic support for Southern blacks, but, as W.E.B. Du Bois and other black radicals pointed out, the psychological cost was high and Southern white aid scant.

WHO INVENTED IT?

193 TRANSISTOR. Source of the electronic revolution, invented at Bell Laboratories by William B. Shockley, John Bardeen, and Walter H. Brattain, in 1947.

194 NYLON. Invented by Wallace Hume Carothers, head of the Du Pont experimental station, in 1937. Nylon stockings came on the market in 1940; they were so popular that Du Pont sold sixty-four million pairs that year. Carothers and his associates at Du Pont also invented the synthetic rubber neoprene.

195 FREQUENCY MODULATION (FM). The system of transmitting sound patterns by varying the frequency of the carrier wave rather than its amplitude (AM), invented by Edwin H. Armstrong in 1933 but not developed widely until after World War II.

196 PERMANENT WAVE. Invented by Karl Ludwig Nessler, a German-born hairdresser, who over a period of years ending in the mid-1920s perfected machines for making hair more porous so that it would absorb moisture. Moist hair holds a curl longer than dry hair, but not, of course, permanently.

Lethal-looking early permanent-wave machine, about 1925.

197 ORAL CONTRACEPTIVE. Invented in the 1950s by Gregory Pincus, who produced Enovid, the first "pill," by combining synthetic progesterone and estrogen.

198 QUICK-FROZEN FOODS. Invented by Clarence Birdseye, who first experimented with the concept while he was a fur trader in Labrador before World War I. Birdseye invented the term *quick-freeze* and sold his patents in 1929.

THE INVENTION THAT WASN'T

199 In the 1870s George B. Selden had developed detailed designs for a "horseless carriage," powered by a gasoline engine and complete with an ignition system, a clutch, brakes, and other details. He never built even a prototype for such a machine, apparently because he was unable to obtain financing. Nevertheless, in 1895 he was issued a patent for a "road engine." He assigned his patent to the Association of Licensed Automobile Manufacturers, and for many years this group licensed the actual manufacture of cars, charging a small royalty. Henry Ford, however, refused to recognize the Selden patent, and in 1911, after a complicated legal battle, a U.S. circuit court decided in Ford's favor.

PHOTO CREDITS

4: University of Hartford Collection, Conn. 11: Culver Pictures
16: Culver Pictures 18: AP/Wide World 25: Carl Iwasaki/*Life* magazine, ©Time Inc. 27: National Archives 28: Schroeder's *The Life
and Times of Washington;* Museum of Fine Arts, Boston; New York
State Historical Association; Metropolitan Musem of Art, New York
City; Kunhardt Collection ; Boston Athenaeum; Harvard University
Library (2) 32: *Puck,*May 16, 1888 34: *Puck,* Mar. 10, 1897
40: Stanley King Collection 46: Division of Political History, Smith-
sonian Institution, Washington, D.C. 57: G.P.A. Healy. Faneuil Hall,
Boston 59: Library of Congress 62: Museum of Fine Arts, Bos-
ton 63: Yale University Art Gallery, New Haven 64: Museum of
Fine Arts, Boston 65: Peale Museum, Baltimore 66: St. Louis Art
Museum 67: Jefferson Medical College, Thomas Jefferson University,
Philadelphia 68: Metropolitan Museum of Art, New York City
69: Cleveland Museum of Art, Hinman B. Hurlbut Collection 70: Art
Institute of Chicago 71: Museum of Modern Art, New York City
96: Library of Congress 98: Henry E. Huntington Library, San
Marino, Calif. 104: Alain Locke, *The New Negro* 115: Brown Brothers 122: New-York Historical Society 129: Erich Hartmann/Mag-
num 131: Culver Pictures (3); UPI/Bettmann; Lincoln Center for
the Performing Arts; UPI/Bettmann (3); AP/Wide World (3); 145: Library of Congress 148: Henry Francis du Pont Winterthur Museum 151: Historical Society of Pennsylvania, Philadelphia
152: New York Public Library, Rare Book Division 153: ©Copy-
righted 1931, Chicago Tribune Co. 154: ©1937 New York News
Inc. 155: St. Louis *Post-Dispatch* 158: National Archives 161: Library of Congress 162: Culver Pictures 164: Brown Brothers
166: Old Print Shop, New York City 168: Private Collection
170: U.S. Naval Institute 171: U.S. Navy 174: Culver Pictures
176: Culver Pictures 180: New-York Historical Society 186: Poster:
Gary Viskupic 188: Pennsylvania Historical and Museum Commission 196: Culver Pictures 199: William R. Ray